Story Teller

Lessons of Joyful Life to be.

LaLit

BookLeaf
Publishing

India | USA | UK

Made with ❤ on the BookLeaf Publishing Platform
www.bookleafpub.in
www.bookleafpub.com

Hey, it's a noticeable act to find whom it is dedicated to.

I have a surprise coming in these poems. It's all about You.

When life comes calling Us' we disguise ourselves in a shell.

It's your dreams shared, how was the experience to be felt.

All dedications are towards successful attempts made for our happiness and filling the hidden gaps of the five fingers.

Enjoy yourself being seen everywhere in the book.

Acknowledgements

Acknowledging my dear ones:

It's a bundle of joyous memories of the loved ones that gracefully took me through this journey.

I had my friends and family around me while my words came free-flowing from their hearts.

Thanks for bringing My Poet in Me

my life partner to be on the top floor to be addressed! Every step of life, she is there.

Every single moment to be cherished.

Many others I ponder with my sincere thanks. Names not to be mentioned; there are a few not to be missed.

A gratifying respect to the publisher who made me become what I am. Without this, it would not happen. All the best make of the book is their expertise.

I thank the Lord for being with Us' Always.

Inside, Outside, Everywhere, Every Moment of Life.

Hope this book helps you gain performance in life.
Thanks to all the readers of this book

Preface

Life stories don't need to be a fantasy fantastic realm, yet if tried from the beginning, they can be a reality. Start slow and nice. Don't haste. Make beautiful steps. Slowly steadily and you will achieve it

1. Age?

This poem celebrates living life fully, free
from the constraints of time and societal
expectations. It encourages embracing joy,
individuality and kindness while staying
youthful in spirit. The poet inspires readers to
shine brightly, cherish each day and create
their own rhythm in life, reminding them
that age is just a number and every moment is
a gift.

Counting backwards,
Time won't wait, won't yield.
Stay bold, stay bright,
Embrace the double – live 48 a day.
Repay your sorrow with joy,
Love your people, your way.

Be blessed, unnumbered,
Full and complete.
Be whole, unsplit–
Be seen, be found,
Be everywhere, not beneath, but around.

Life isn't a measure,
It's not a race.
Be kind, not in haste;
For the future, stay here – present today.
Be of a kind, pay no mind,
Let your essence be the sign.

Why so serious?
Why the worry?
Why so many fears,
When 'why not me' can lead?
Why not solo? Why not free?
Why not 'we'?

For you are timeless,
Not bound, not aged.
Stay young, stay fresh,
Be the mesh – filter the waste,

And blossom in gold.

Feel no cold, radiate heat,
Be the rhythm, the beat.
You belong to no tribe,
You're your own vibe.

Every day's a birthday,
Some things never fade.
Shine bright, eternal–
A star, forever made.

2. Ann2

This poem explores a deep and transformative connection between two souls. It begins with sensual imagery, symbolising intimacy and passion, but quickly transitions to a higher, more profound bond – one of unity, respect and mutual growth. The relationship is described as pure, unburdened by societal expectations and rooted in love, pride and joy. It celebrates individuality within togetherness, portraying a connection that is both spiritual and grounded in the simplicity of shared moments. Ultimately, it's a tribute to a love that is tender, enduring and uniquely fulfilling.

Dip in softly, feel the tide,
Dive down deep where secrets hide.
Slip through gullies, taste the sea,
Breath held tight, just you and me.
Waves that drench, a steamy trance,
Sweat and water in a dance.

Provocative,
Voluptuous,
A moment – so sumptuous.

Boldly tracing every line,
Curves that meet, our hearts align.
But wait – no!

This is not us.

Gentle, sweet and gratifying,
Minds in flight, souls unifying.
A bond that bewilders, a world we create,
Glamorous love that defies its fate.
Never weary,

Never torn,
No regrets – just love reborn.

We bloom like buds in morning's glow,
Transform into flowers as rivers flow.
A journey slow, yet wholly ours,
Two become one beneath the stars.

Paranormal in a mundane sphere,
A love so true, so proud, so sincere.
Nurturing joy in every stride,
A convoy bound for endless pride.
No need for others, no crutch, no guise,
Just us alone beneath wide skies.

Carefree surrender,
Soft and tender.
Sober yet playful,
Feelings so grateful.

Besties we are,
Through highs and lows,
Through gentle tides and storms that rose.

Let me kneel, to kiss your feet,

A vow of love, both strong and sweet.
No bows, no chains, no rigid creed,
Only respect, the love we need.

Not too serious,
Not too light,
Separate souls,
Yet so tight.

We are the rhythm, the breath, the song,
Together alive, where we belong.

3. Newly Forming Couples
Double Us' is the Sync

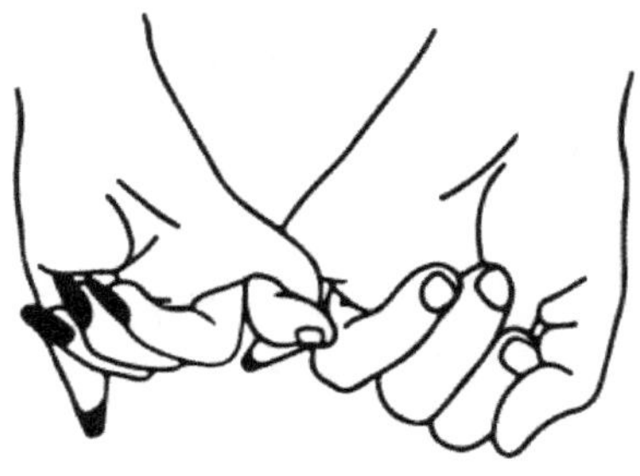

I believed in you because I wanted to overcome the belief in myself better. When it's us, it brings a smile of being ONE.

The gap of separation will be coming & going always.

Hence, when I bring you in, then I have no fear of that kind of gap.

Hiccups will be there.
When we will believe in ONE SouL, then the rest of the world won't affect Us'

It's a practice to believe
It's a practice to achieve
When we will achieve
Then there will be nothing to scare us or
bother us anymore

Hence, the speed of un-limiting ourselves
should be a running desire
Mind is the culprit
Heart is the SouL.

Have to believe and practice to be the master
of the SouL and not the mind.

4. Newly Formed Couples: Double Us' is the Goal

I believed in you to break my shell,
To rise where my own faith fell.
When it's Us, it feels complete,
A bond where heart and echoes meet.

The gaps of time may drift, may sway,
Yet love won't turn or fade away.
For when I hold you deep inside,
No space can shake, no fear divide.

Yes, trials come some hard to bear,
But souls as One can clear the air.
We practice trust, we practice grace,
And fear will never haunt this space.

So let's run wild, unchained, untamed,
With dreams too vast to be explained.
For hearts, not minds, should take control
The mind's a thief, the heart's the Soul.

5. Sync'

Between the years, through time we flow,
A secret world where echoes grow.
It matters not where footsteps roam
For Us together feels like home.

Be it near or far away,
A dream, a trip, or just today.
The thrill's in going, free from chains,
The fear of not a fleeting pain.

Double the day, Double the night,
Double the sparks that burn so bright.
Moments pass but can't outshine,
The joy we feel when hearts entwine.

An hour or two.. just passing shows,

But planning's where the magic grows.
For even when the time is small,
We share the love that holds it all.

6. The Game of Us

And if we are to cross that space,
Let's make it swift ..let's set the pace.
Live the joy for just one day,
Then double it without delay.

Two turns six oh, let it rise!
A love that lifts, a life that flies.
To multiply what's real and true,
Is Us, unbound just me and you.

No guilt, no fear, no holding back,
No maps to trace, no beaten track.
Just endless Us, where hearts run free ..
Un-limiting Us, infinitely!

7. It's a story of ki & ka

Like Ki Nai' & Ka Yes'

This poem seemingly captures the complexity of a relationship, possibly referencing a dynamic between two people symbolised by 'ki & ka' and 'K___ Nai & K'___Yes'. The use of phrases like 'B'ay', 'stars and gifts for a deer babe' and 'camouflag'e' suggests a whimsical, almost dreamlike narrative that plays with language and meaning.

The poem appears to depict a series of emotional shifts and moments of connection, starting with confusion (NOoOOoOo comes first), followed by clarity (Yes comes then) and then a reversal of events (point no. 5 whole story reverses again). There's a sense of disorientation but also a sense of shared affection (Cuddles in bundles for buddies they were), with the ups and downs of a relationship.

The mention of 'toast' and 'secluded things' might represent intimate, celebratory moments, but there are also doubts and conflicts (Doubts and Cuts go creepy with her when he calls a crap). The 'crescent' may symbolise fluctuating emotions or phases, suggesting both an internal struggle (Virtual it is and real me instead) and the challenge of understanding each other (Who will understand their under-liners here).

Overall, the poem explores the complexity of a relationship, filled with moments of joy, confusion, celebration and conflict, all

conveyed through fragmented language and
imagery.

15.9 starts with a B'ay.
Or with stars and gifts for a deer babe.

Starters were camouflag'e What's a. And
what's a koala
Are they some flags!!

NOoOOoOo comes first and Yes comes then
When comes point no. 5, whole story reverses
again

Who tells sara and all with a para but who
tells no with all one a sign go somewhere with
no clue there...

Cuddles in bundles for buddies they were
Super nice stories shared forever

Then comes a toast when B'ay hits on
then,

With secluded things & SoH with them.

Doubts and Cuts go creepy with her when he
calls a crap and bumpy for sure.

Crescent is coming and going in the head.
Virtual it is and real me instead

Who will understand their under-liners here?
It's ki and ka to define the den!

8. Price to Priceless

The first invoice bore your V.O.I.C.E,
A melody rich, a love so precise.
Then came the GST talks, laughs, and fights,
Moments that turned to endless delights.

You gave your love with no demand,
While fools still weigh it in coin and hand.
But you knew well what's given returns,
In abundance as the heart sojourns.

Your S.M.I.L.E the sweetest rebate,
A tax waiver time cannot negate.
I hoard them now in endless stores,
Priceless treasures forevermore.
This heavy package lifts my soul,
What debt to charge when you've made me
whole?
One more FY of life, I plead,
To pay you back in word and deed.

I brim with profits your love untold,
Yet balance my sheet in wealth of gold.
An endless affair, no loss, no gain
Just love in surplus, timely again.

9. Feel' forever

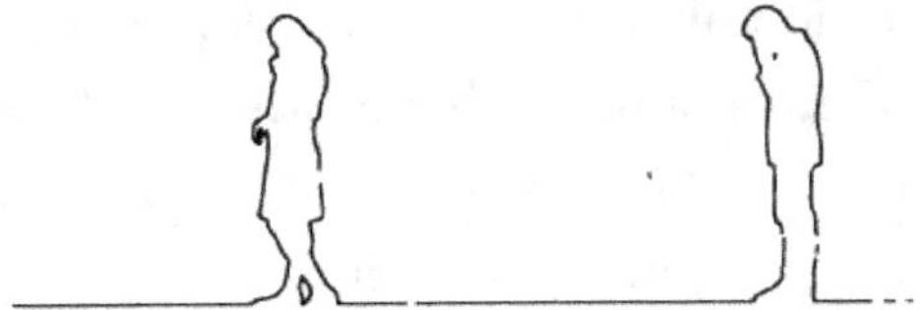

This poem expresses the contrast between two emotional states within a relationship – bliss and blush – and the desire for those feelings to remain unchanged. The speaker acknowledges that their emotions (blush) are different from the other person's (bliss), yet they yearn for a deep connection where both can feel each other's emotions, even if they are not the same.

The repetition of 'Let it not happen, Let it not go away' expresses a longing to preserve this feeling forever, emphasising the desire for an enduring, unbroken connection. 'Feel forever it is' conveys a sense of timelessness, with the speaker wanting to keep the emotion of 'blush' and the other person's 'bliss' as eternal.

The mention of 'Valentine's forever' ties the poem to love, romantic affection and the celebration of lasting feelings, suggesting that this connection, much like Valentine's Day, should be enduring and special, beyond just a moment in time.

Overall, the poem is a meditation on love, the beauty of emotional contrasts and the wish for a timeless bond.

The way I feel is not the way I want you to feel

You remain in bliss forever
I remain in blush forever

Your bliss & my blush are different and I feel you to feel me like' whenever

Let it not happen
Let it not go away
Let it be forever

Let it be this feel

Feel forever it is...
Is my forever blush
Is your forever bliss

Valentines 💌 Forever
It is.

10. No gifts are they... to open & spy. Here's the secret not to deny

This poem seems to explore the themes of love, admiration and the exchange of intangible gifts that hold deeper meaning. The speaker expresses that material gifts are not the true treasures, but rather, there are secret, meaningful tokens exchanged between the speaker and the loved one.

The 'Moroccan Mirror' is symbolic, possibly representing a reflection of the person's true self or a deeper connection, while 'Stars to keep you glittery' suggests that the person is a source of light and wonder. The fragrance represents a gift that's meant to be passed on, perhaps symbolising something fleeting but meaningful.

The mention of the moon suggests a connection to something eternal and unshakeable (No one steals her ever Again), implying loyalty or protection. The 'chain' might represent a bond or connection that is meant to keep the loved one close, though it contrasts with the more delicate affection ('UnLike the hug you give me slighter).

The poem then delves into the idea of love as an exchange that's not just material (Dollars honey were exchange back offers), but one that also has depth, as shown in the metaphors of the 'Dragon' and 'butterfly'. The speaker seems to suggest they embody strength and protection (Dragon was Me not the fly), while the loved one embodies beauty and grace ('butterfly Miss' HigH).

The final line, 'Chocolates only. Left for you. Be gifting. As perfect as you', suggests that simple gestures, like gifting chocolates, are enough to express affection, as they are

imbued with love and appreciation,
symbolising sweetness and care.

Overall, the poem conveys the sentiment that
the most meaningful gifts in love are not
always physical but are found in gestures,
symbols and the deep, intangible connection
between two people.

Moroccan Mirror to watch your Eye Circle.
Stars to keep you glittery, you are a found
miracle

Fragrance was a return pass it on as well …zzz
Though all this I couldn't really tell.

The Moon kept with Me* for game.
No one steals her ever
Again

The chain was to arm you tighter & tighter
UnLike the hug you give me slighter!

Dollars honey were exchange back offers.
To pump on gold for the stockers

Dragon was Me, not the fly
To keep a blue eye on your butterfly 🦋 Miss'
HigH.

Chocolates ◆ only.
Left for you
Be gifting
As perfect as you.

11. Piya re...

This poem is a tribute to a strong, inspiring
and graceful woman, using vivid imagery and
metaphors to highlight her beauty, strength
and multifaceted nature. The speaker praises
her as 'beautiful as Fairy', 'talented as she
deserves' and 'charming as Mother Mary',
suggesting she possesses an otherworldly
elegance and nurturing qualities. The phrase
'Me ready to ReMarry' implies a deep
admiration, as though the speaker would
choose her over and over again.

Despite facing tough times, the woman is
depicted as resilient and graceful (She knows
to tie her laces when time comes bad she

embraces), embracing challenges with strength and poise. The poem repeatedly emphasises her various roles – 'a figure', 'a fighter', 'laughter' and 'a flier' – indicating her dynamic presence.

The woman is also described as a source of beauty and influence (Spreading fashion, Colorful Fabric on our lives she is), showing her impact on the lives of others. The closing lines, 'Be with her, Be her, Be blessed', suggest that being in her presence is a gift and a blessing.

Overall, the poem celebrates this woman's resilience, charm and transformative influence, elevating her to an almost mythical level. It conveys deep admiration and respect for her strength, beauty and ability to inspire.

Beautiful as Fairy
Talented as She Deserves.
Me ready to ReMarry

The flying fairy she is.

Charming as Mother Mary
With her lads
Both to carry.

Smooth sailing she is...
–although Tough times act she faces
She knows to tie her laces
When times come bad she embraces

A Figure she is
Fighter she is
Laughter she is
A Flier she is

Spreading fashion
She is
Colorful Fabric on our lives she is

Be with her
Be her
Be blessed

Regards,

6moReShoTs##
She is.

12. Ann23

This poem reflects on the challenges and complexities of a relationship, possibly focusing on the dynamics between two people over time. The 'duplex' suggests shared living spaces or lives, while the 'repercussions' hint at the struggles and tensions that can arise between partners. The speaker expresses a sense of disconnect, with romance pushed aside due to 'petty works' and coldness in the relationship.

The mention of '22 to hold' and 'waiting for the gold' may symbolise a time of patience, where the speaker is waiting for something better to emerge, such as a reward or resolution. 'Break line on 25' implies a turning point or moment of relief, perhaps a break in the tension, and a chance for celebration.

The lines about losing and finding love suggest a cycle of ups and downs in the relationship, but the focus is on letting go of overthinking (remove the overthinking heads) and simplifying communication. The reference to a 'Ted Talk' could symbolise open, honest conversations, while 'picnic point' suggests that fun and connection come when things are light-hearted and free from overanalysis.

The final lines evoke a desire for the simplicity and joy of the past, asking for 'mornings back to stay', signalling a longing for the days when things felt easier and more connected.

Overall, the poem is a meditation on the tension between the complexities of life and relationships and the yearning to reclaim simpler, more joyous moments together. The link at the end could relate to a specific moment of reflection or inspiration tied to the poem.

It's come over ages
Spending time with
A duplex

When the repercussions come to shadow your partnership. Feel like overdoing some joy. What the other partner wants is still a lot mystery to solve the ploy

Lot many petty works to finish makes the romance kept aside
Its cold here by the side

It's 22 to hold
And wait for the gold

It's a break line on 25 to rejoice the party
affair to Mould

Bring the party and the people for
celebrations with others
Bring the moments of us being celebrated
together whether?
Not with our feathers

Losing the love to find back and track
Needs no meditation struggle on your back

We simply remove the over thinking heads
And bond free the speech laying our Ted

Talks not necessarily make your joint
Fun goes when it's a picnic point

Steadily slowly fading away. Bring the
mornings back to stay

https://www.instagram.com/reel/DCXqIjaKS
W4/?igsh=OHowcjF6NDZ3N3Y3

13. Love is abundance

Like is Limited

This poem contrasts the concepts of love and like, emphasising the depth, permanence and selflessness of love compared to the temporary and often superficial nature of like. It begins by illustrating love as abundant, blind and unconditional, while like is limited, sighted and conditional. The poem highlights the difference in emotional weight, stating that love is heavy and eternal, while like is light and fleeting.

Love is described as something that is one-of-a-kind and can't be undone, whereas like can be reversed. Love is portrayed as the more profound emotion – full of sacrifice, pain and growth – while like is simply a fleeting, surface-level feeling. The poem also plays on the idea of actions: in love, one hides their true feelings, while in like, there's more show and boasting. Ultimately, the poem suggests that while likes may come and go, love remains eternal and even starts from a place of love.

It underscores that love is the foundation, while like is just a part of that larger, infinite connection.

Love is blind
Like is sighted

You can Unlike
But there is nothing
Called UnLove.

Love is non-returnable
Like is a return gift

Love is heavy
Like is Light

Like is me
Love is U.

Like has memories
Love is forever

Like is beautiful
Love is Larger Than Life

Like is fun & over
Love is just the beginning
To no end.

Likes are many
Love is One

Like is painless
Love hurts

Like is Hug
Hug is Love

Like is conditional
Love is Not

In Like you Show
In Love you Hide

In Like you Boast
In Love you Shy

Likes are in days
Love is Immortal

Love Can't stop
Like starts with Love

14. Sorry I am…

This poem reflects feelings of regret, loss and self-discovery. The speaker apologises for changes in their behaviour, relationships and sense of self. There's a deep sense of confusion and sorrow as they express how they've lost their way – once vibrant and full of life, now detached and uncertain. They mourn the absence of past connections and experiences, like the fading of a relationship or the loss of their former selves. The speaker's apologies reveal a longing for understanding and a desire for reconciliation, while also acknowledging the inevitable transformations that come with time and change. Ultimately, the poem conveys the complexity of personal evolution and the emotional struggle that comes with it.

Not to be Me
Sorry I am that I stopped watching U'Moon

Sorry I am not to see you as U' like before. I
am lost. Like I lost my hak@chair hak@hug
sophomore

Sorry to be busy again and to be like an ugly
me.

I am sorry can't find my mirror
And no importance to see
Me

Sorry not to be crazy again and be normal
bending on my knee.
Sorry I was Krishna
And now my face off is left with only me!

Sorry to build memories and vanish like were
never before
I am sorry for no gifts, no me' nothing from
me

I am Sorry not to find myself And seems a
dream to me.

Sorry proving everyone wrong
And being a Sole Follower and now
unfollowing you to me

Though I couldn't be a buddy
...give me a chance to be just a friend &
uncuddle me.

Sorry didn't even realise.
both disappeared
Butterfly turned to caterpillars thee'

Ki & Ka broke up after years
Sorry for not to patch up again.
...we.
Sorry not to understand the difference
between the busyness & the change!
Sorry I invented a dot.
But didn't know to use it spot.
Sorry to be 'not me'.

15. Shuttle to Closed Shutters

This poem expresses deep emotional turmoil and the end of a significant relationship or bond, perhaps a friendship. The opening lines, 'When shutters close / & Hearts open', suggest a moment of emotional vulnerability or a shift in feelings. The 'rumbles around / Ringing bells in the ground' could symbolise inner turmoil or conflict, leading to the speaker feeling 'Frozen' and 'Deep Broken'.

The lines 'No one to stand / They Can't understand' imply isolation and a lack of support, with the phrase 'Say' Stop forever / Our friendship is over' marking a definitive end. The speaker then expresses a sense of emotional numbness, with phrases like 'We no hurt / We don't hurt' and 'Stay away on earth', as if distancing themselves from the pain or the relationship altogether.

The poem reflects confusion and resignation – 'No ray of hope / To climb the rope' – and a feeling of being stuck in a situation with no growth (No plant to grow). The absence of 'cuddles' and emotional closeness points to the coldness and distance that have taken over.

However, there is also a theme of forgiveness and purity (Pure we souL / Forgive them whole), indicating a desire to let go of bitterness and move on from the pain. The poem ends with an enigmatic line, 'Do Screen & Scroll / Sure Will find 'no' Coal', suggesting that searching for negativity or holding on to anger only leads to further emptiness, as symbolised by the absence of 'Coal'.

Overall, the poem conveys the pain of loss, the struggle to understand the end of a relationship and the internal conflict between

holding onto hurt and seeking forgiveness
and healing.

When shutters close
& Hearts open
Rumbles around
Ringing bells in the ground
Until I Frozen
Deep Broken

No one to stand
They Can't understand
Say' Stop forever
Our friendship is over

We no hurt
We don't hurt
Thee see dirt
Stay away on earth

No ray of hope
To climb the rope

Twinkle nope
Trigger me slow
Scary though

No bad deed
Y Punished me slow
Say What's wrong dude
Go with the flow
Where can we sow
No plant to grow

Just buddies were we
No cuddles were been
Do u all know
Nothing to be told
Nothing was before
Nothing ever more
What touched your core
Never had a score

Scars left behind.
Separate mind
Secret of a kind
Wrongly defined

Pure we souL
Forgive them whole
Spare the voLe
You make us stole
Do Screen & Scroll
Sure Will find 'no' Coal

16. Naive'

This poem is a heartfelt tribute to someone the speaker admires deeply, focusing on their inner and outer beauty as well as their character. The speaker describes the person as 'smart, beautiful and sexy', highlighting their charm, lovability and all-around positive qualities. The line 'the most gorgeous & amazing buddy bee'! emphasises the closeness of their bond and the affection the speaker feels.

The poem encourages the person to continue being themselves – 'Smiling as always you been' – and to remain as bright and radiant as they naturally are, comparing their energy to the warmth of sunshine and the sparkle of moonlight. There's a focus on purity, honesty and emotional depth, praising the person for their emotional and devotional nature.

The speaker wishes the person happiness and success, offering a 'gentle hug' and affirming that their connection is lasting, with no 'farewell ever ever'. This gives a sense of eternal support and friendship, with the speaker expressing their desire for the person to continue shining and succeeding in life.

Overall, the poem conveys a deep sense of admiration, affection and unwavering friendship, celebrating the person's qualities while wishing them a lifetime of happiness and fulfilment.

Yet smart
Beautiful and Sexy U'

...Charming and Lovable. And much more
too! Be.
...the most gorgeous & amazing buddy bee!
Wishes across my heart
Straight to your souL
Don't they apart.

Be like you are
Smiling as always you been.
Bright like sunshine
Sparkling like moonlight, it's keen.

Be pure, be innocent
Be true, be honest
Be the best of you
As you always do.

Emotional and devotional are both your
mind. What a blend you have got in mankind.

Wish you loads of happiness
from within!
A gentle hug from a Buddy Friend you win...
Roll & Rock your way up clever
...Lifetime yours forever with

no, no farewell ever, ever...ever.

17. Ache in the pain

Though Beauty of Her is there

This poem seems to explore themes of strength, defiance and the complex nature of relationships, particularly between sisters or close companions. The speaker addresses someone, possibly with a sense of playful warning, suggesting a mix of affection and toughness. The opening lines – 'Touch me not sweety / Will kill you in vain' suggest a boundary that should not be crossed, hinting at both emotional and physical strength.

The next lines, 'Don't shout loud / Don't bark foul', imply the speaker is not easily intimidated, and they may respond more forcefully (am@ / Louder than you scout). The reference to 'Shambhu' (a name that could allude to Lord Shiva) and 'hird eye outside' suggests a deeper awareness or perception, with a spiritual undertone.

The lines 'Soft tissue breed / Hard butter seed' evoke a contrast between softness and toughness, possibly symbolising the speaker's inner complexity – gentle yet resilient. The 'Melting pot' line hints at vulnerability or transformation but with a warning not to 'get caught'.

The mention of 'Disciplined brown girl / English way she's curled' seems to describe the speaker or the subject as someone who is both grounded in their cultural roots and shaped by external influences or discipline.

Finally, the lines 'Love her she loves you / Scratch her she bites you' convey the dual nature of this person – affectionate yet capable of fierce retaliation, suggesting that relationships can be both nurturing and intense, with boundaries that should be respected.

Overall, the poem reflects a playful yet assertive personality, exploring the complex nature of love, strength and the consequences of crossing certain lines.

Touch me not sweety
Will kill you in vain

Don't shout loud
Don't bark foul
Hehe otherwise am@
Louder than you scout

Shambhu inside
Third eye outside
Soft tissue breed
Hard butter seed

Melting pot
Don't get caught

Fight me out
I am tired of spout

Disciplined brown girl
English way she's curled

Love her she loves you
Scratch her she bites you

18. Unapologetic

Am I. Little.

This poem explores themes of self-identity, introspection and emotional strength. The speaker reflects on their past and present selves, expressing defiance and a refusal to apologise for who they are. The repetition of 'Am I' highlights a struggle with self-definition, while the lines about being 'Unapologetic' suggest a desire to break free from past expectations or guilt. The speaker rejects external judgements and embraces a sense of inner power and resilience, finding strength in their own evolving identity. Overall, the poem speaks to the journey of self-acceptance and the complexity of navigating one's emotional and mental landscape.

Learnt to be warned
before: " . "
mind becomes mindless
When night becomes sleepless
& mornings go soundless
There is enough room to
groom* after the before#

Unspeakable
Am I today
Thoughtless
Am I today
Ruthless
Am I today

Unapologetically
Was I before
Wrong was I before
Strong was I before
I have to do nothing
Before.

Never hurt your feelings

Before
Never strain your brain
Before
Never asked you fall
Before

Refreshing a month, says my dear,
Be guilt-free a little
Cheer up a little
Jingle a little

O my Me Alone...
Not used to this mental
Makes me more brittle
Was So pleased to
Spend a little
Give a little

I am a Man of More
I am Merrier than my
Own Score
Stopping Me
Will Vulcanise & Pour
Don't let the Sun come to the Shore!

Shutters will close a little
Waters won't melt a little

19. Waqt ka dariya hai Jo Dooriya bada tha hai

This poem reflects the feelings of longing and hope amidst separation. The speaker expresses that despite the distance created by time (Waqt ka dariya hai), the absence of the other person doesn't bring sorrow because the memories serve as a source of strength to keep going. There's a sense of optimism in the belief that someone else, perhaps even more caring and beautiful than the person being addressed, may come into the speaker's life, bringing with them a sense of renewal and movement (mera thehra hua sama phir se chal padega).

The speaker acknowledges the presence of the other person's shadow in their life, and even in their absence, they hope that someone similar will take care of them in the same way. This poem is a bittersweet reflection on love, loss and the possibility of future connections, highlighting both the pain of separation and the enduring hope of finding comfort once again.

Varna Tu nahi tho bhi koi gam nahi
Teri yadoon ke Sahaare jeena seekh lunga

Aur phir kya pata
Koi tho 8 wa ajooba aapke jaisa mere Samne
ajay ga
Aur mera thehra hua sama Phir se chal
padega

Jo aapke jaise khubsoorat hoga aur app se
jyaada mera khayal rakhega

Bus kya kahoon mein ab

Aapki parchaiye banke ayega

62

20. BoOoOo

My Sis

This poem playfully describes the speaker's sister, highlighting both her strong and gentle qualities in a whimsical and fun tone. The speaker depicts the sister as someone who navigates a 'scary world' with confidence, strength and individuality. She's portrayed as both fierce (bossy, touchy) and fragrant, with references to her essence, likening her to divine figures like 'Shivshamboo' and 'VishBoo'.

The poem contrasts her multifaceted nature – while she may be shy at times, she's also full of

surprises, capable of shocking others with her actions. There's a playful element to the sister's affection, represented by the 'loves me, loves me not' game, a recurring theme that reflects the ups and downs of their sibling bond. Ultimately, the poem celebrates the sister's complexity, her charm and the deep love between them.
It's a scary world for a girL.
For the betterment of her
She fights the CurL

Already The 'Wonderful' she is
Don't Wonder her steady
Bossy she is.
Don't angry me.
Touchy she is.
Don't finger me.

Shivshamboo she is.
VishBoo she is.
Fragrance, ask me, unlimited
When khushboo she is.

Child Chapter she is
A Tutorial Lesson she is.
When Shubh she is
SHUBH mangal it is.
Shy He is, that's Y not she is.

Attractive she is, though
...Gale Lag ja... then,
How Shocking she is.
Whisper her, then a sweet surprise She is.

She loves me
She loves me not
She loves me
She loves me not
She loves me
She loves me not

...

21. T & J...

Long-wed Couple

This poem humorously portrays the dynamics of a long-married couple, symbolised by the famous cartoon characters Tom and Jerry. Jerry (J) represents the mischievous one, while Tom (T) is the more serious or 'slamming' counterpart. The mother figure, akin to a "super furious mom," is the one who keeps order in the household, especially after Jerry's antics with the gong. The playful narrative revolves around the couple's ups and downs – Jerry causing chaos and Tom trying to restore calm – all while the mom supervises with a mix of frustration and affection.

The poem touches on the resilience of the couple's bond, likening their relationship to a merry-go-round and highlighting how they navigate life together, even when apart. Despite their differences, they come together to 'sing a family song', emphasising unity, love and shared experiences.

The light-hearted tone conveys that, like any family, they endure ups and downs with humour and warmth, and with the blessings of time, their journey continues – new stories emerge, symbolised by the transition from childhood to maturity. The playful, comedic atmosphere is reinforced by the acknowledgement of the family's shared 'secret recipe' for staying together.

Characters: Tom & Jerry
Directors: The family
Comedian: The mom
Action: Jerry
Music: Comedy vibes
Lyricist: Lalit

The poem concludes with a note of ongoing adventure, making it clear that the family's story never truly ends.

J is for Jerry
T is Tom
The great mom in their big house with a big gong.

...Beneath run J
Above slams the Tom
She, Super furious Mom
After Jerry rang the bong
Ding dong ding dong.

To be a Surprise for her
He went rallying above the roads of Tung
Finished his flag winning red cheeks angering her aboard... how many to keep the Kumbh!!
Run J run after she comes
Run Jerry run after Mom succumbs

Bhaag Milkha Bhaag
It is. A Merry go Round

GeL they when things apart
Paste they when we a part
Party kept all year round
Secret recipe is to bond

Together they sing a family song
You can't hear... be along

May Lord bless them with
Cheer and Gear
& serious it is when it comes to their little
one to glare

With life & glory
Comes the next story...
A Clay lover becomes a young vibe... glads
Lori

Never the end!

Characters: Tom & Jerry
Directors: the family Comedian: the mom
parent
Action: Jerry

Music: Comedy Vibes
Lyricist: Lalit

22. Fearless Lad 18

This poem celebrates the journey of growth, self-realisation and the fearless pursuit of one's goals. The speaker reflects on the fear of becoming fearless and the transformation it brings – acknowledging the many achievements, relationships and experiences that shape a person. As the 'fearless lad' turns 18, the poem highlights the strength and confidence gained through overcoming challenges. The speaker emphasises the power of responsibility, respect and humanity, portraying the individual as someone who has evolved into a mature and accomplished person, ready to take on the world. The poem ends on a note of pride and accomplishment,

showing how far the 'lad' has come in his
journey.

Have you ever thought the fear of being
fearless

The longevity mind towards the
accomplishment of the rainbow in you.
All sudden, All Colors of the Worlds come
together for you to ReveaL
Books
Trip
Party
Friends
Family
Goals Achieved in
Every Game of Journey

The fearless you became
The Unstoppable you are.
Speeding 18
Lightening inside
Silent outside

Audible Hearable are you.

Now is the beginning...
Of birds & the bees.
From every country
Of the world to acknowledge
To Court of a justifiable life

Tall as a giraffe
Tall as a father figure
He has All in His Call

Call of Duty
Call of Responsibility
Call of Respect
Call of Humanity

It's Been You zzz
A Lad
A Freind
A Today
An Achiever

23. Lover Lover

This poem expresses deep love, admiration and devotion to a partner. The speaker reflects on the powerful connection they share with their lover, emphasising how she is a constant presence in their life – guiding, comforting and offering stability. The imagery of love as a sanctuary, a place of peace, and a source of strength highlights the transformative power of their bond.

The speaker celebrates the many facets of their relationship: from shared dreams and tender moments to overcoming challenges together. The lover is described as both fierce and nurturing, someone who helps the speaker find peace, erase doubts and embrace love fully. The poem concludes with a commitment to the enduring nature of their love, valuing simplicity, companionship and mutual respect and declaring their love as a source of strength and growth.

Overall, the poem is a beautiful tribute to a relationship built on trust, passion and unwavering support, with the promise of a love that will continue to thrive.

In the realm where belief and hope collide,
A love blossoms, where hearts confide.
She's always by my side, a constant guide,
In her embrace, love's truth shall reside.

With her, moments of togetherness unfold,
Sharing dreams, as love's stories are told.
Her caring touch, a warmth to behold,
She's the essence of love, a love so bold.

Her spirit gallops like rolling mists,
Stable and serene, where peace persists.
Longing to stay, in love's sweet tryst,

She's mighty, a love that truly insists.

In prayer's sanctuary, we find our grace,
Sharing suppers, our souls interlace.
She's the one who stops my restless chase,
With her, my doubts and fears erase.

Forever available, a love that won't fade,
A friend, a buddy, in every escapade.
A companion, through light and shade,
With her, a love story that will never degrade.

She's a fighter, with a fiery soul,
An angry woman who makes me whole.
We take oaths, as our love unfolds,
In her dominion, a love story to extol.

So let's be safe in love's sweet embrace,
Embrace simplicity, let worries erase.
With her, we're sure, our love's base,
Together we thrive, in this enchanted space.

In every moment, let's be there,
As pals, as lovers, a bond beyond compare.
Honoring her, a love we both share,

True being, her love forever we declare.

24. Celeb@40

This poem celebrates the milestone of turning 40, capturing the excitement and joy of reflecting on the years lived and looking forward to the future. The speaker expresses a sense of pride and youthful energy as they approach this age, seeing it as an opportunity for continued growth, fun and achievement. There's a light-hearted tone throughout, with references to staying young, adventurous and 'naughty' at 40, emphasising that age is just a number and doesn't define one's vitality or spirit. The poem is a playful and celebratory reflection on the journey of life, filled with optimism and a commitment to living fully.

It feels like celebration for self with cheers
Lots of excitement to go everywhere
Lots of fun to imagine there

Let's do this and let's do that.
What a great time to achieve in a stat.

I am still young and full of life absorption.
May I have the best prime of My* portion

Counting dreams to that number 39. Oops!
here comes sooner, the 40th. Mine.

Stay blessed forever
Stay young forever
Stay tuned forever
Stay naughty 40! Ever.

25. I hate you

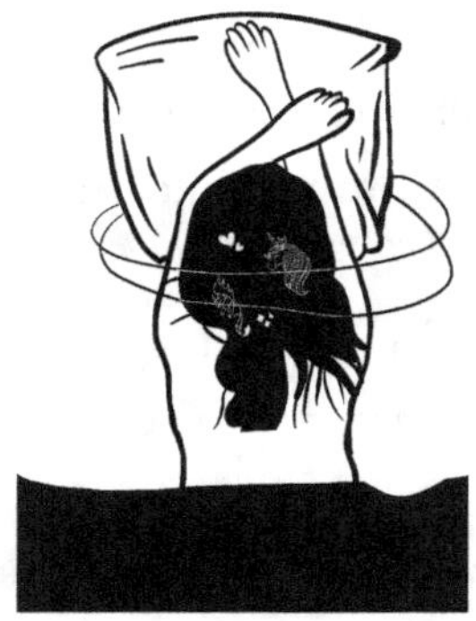

I hate you for saying sorry and not 'love you'

I hate you for not disturbing me and teasing
me all over

I hate you for sending few a pic and not a
collage of pics everyday

I hate you when you say I like your way and
not love your way

I hate you when you cry
And not come to me when you need me the
most.

I hate you when you hide your sorrows and
not to tell me any.

I hate you for giving arms and being shy to
completely hug me

I hate you when you smile and not scold me
for my actions or misbehavior

I hate you for surrendering yourself inspite
me surrendering to you

I hate you for being so kind and caring and
not hating me for anything

I love you in any form
I love the most of you
I love you being loved
I love you grow more
I love your every pic
I love your every style
I love you in all kinds

26. Neha, my Wife...

Jo kam bole, woh hai Neha,
Jo gossip na samjhe, wah Neha.
Jo chinta na kare, woh hai Neha,
Jo kam muskuraye, woh hai Neha.
Jo kam jaane, woh hai Neha,
Jo ginti mein na ho, woh hai Neha,
Line ke peeche khadi reh jaye, woh hai Neha.

To phir, kya hai Neha?

Jo khul ke hase, woh hai Neha,
Jise samajhna chahiye, woh hai Neha.
Line mein aage khud hi aaye, woh hai Neha.

Jo chinta nahi, sidha malam lagaye,
Meri Zandu Balm hai Neha.

Jo sirf kaam kare, seva mein jatan kare,
Woh hai Neha.
Baatein kam, action zyada,
Chhoti khwahishein, bade jazbaat,
Woh hai Neha.

Chhote sapne, par khubsoorat swab v,
Woh hai Neha.
Godmother hai Neha,
Superpower hai Neha.
Rukna nahi aata use,
Bas chalte jaana jaane Neha.

Sabko khilaye, sabko bhaaye,
Sabka saath nibhaane wali,
Woh hai Neha.

Sab uske saath khush rehte,
Gam ko door kare,
Woh hai Neha.

Meri lazy morning hai Neha,

Meri ghar ki baarish hai Neha.
Hamaari trip ki planner hai Neha.

Kya kahoon, bas itna samajh lo–
Japte hai mala jiski,
Zindagi ki raftaar hai Neha.

Courtesy:
I express, she's unimpressed.
I love, she hates.
I relax, she wonders.
I play, she doesn't.
I'm calm, she's hot.
I pamper, she hits.

She cooks, I bake.
She eats, I feed.
She bounces, I lose.
She ounces, I win.

27. JiL the chapter

Your poem reimagines Jack and Jill with a modern, whimsical twist. Jill is portrayed as a dynamic, magical and independent figure – a 'queen of dreams' and master of her own journey. Jack plays a supportive role, complementing her boldness. The narrative blends themes of adventure, individuality and the strength of their unique bond. It's a playful celebration of Jill's vibrant energy and Jack's steadfast presence.

JacK & JiL went up the hill to fetch a board of
gamer.

JiL caMe doWn
To roLL the croWn
And JacK came tumbling after.

Queen of dreams
Merry go round
She needs a band
Of Laughter

JiL is JiL
Keep her chiLL
And see the magic
Go after...

When you saiL with
Her carder slots
No one to compare
Her chapteR

Once she is high
Go beat her by
I bet you shy

She is House ka rafteR

Seen her before
As a drafter crafter
When she was a Master...
Leave her away

To go her way
Be jacK besides safeR
As a LofteR

Sweet surprise
JiL
Heavy package jacK
Be the bonding after.

Dreamscape
Landscape
Full scape...
JiL the chapter.